# THE VOICE IN MY HAND:
# LESSONS

# IN

*LaDora White McDaniel*

# THE VOICE IN MY HAND
# LESSONS
## IN
# *L*OVE

LEIA'S LEGACY BOOKS

2025

THE CONTENTS ARE DEDICATED TO THE PEOPLE I HAVE
MET ALONG THE WAY. ESPECIALLY TO THE ONES THAT
ENCOURAGED ME TO PUT SOMETHING ON PAPER THEY
CAN ENJOY.

LOVE YOU
D

## NOTE FROM THE POET

MY HAND IS HOW I SPEAK TO YOU
IN A CROWD OR ALONE
THE WORDS FROM MY HAND WILL BE WITH YOU LONG
AFTER I AM GONE

MY HAND HOLDS THE PEN
THAT CAN TAKE YOU ANYWHERE
THE VOICE IN MY HEART MY HAND CAN SHARE

WORDS THAT CANNOT COME FROM MY LIPS REST IN MY
FINGERTIPS
MY HAND IS HOW I SPEAK TO YOU
LISTEN TO THE VOICE IN MY HAND

*LaDora White McDaniel*

*"LaDee"*

# TABLE OF CONTENTS

# TABLE OF CONTENTS

# TABLE OF CONTENTS

# TABLE OF CONTENTS

# THE VOICE IN MY HAND:
# LESSONS
# IN

# FLOWERING LOVE

LOVE IS LIKE A BLOOMING
FLOWER.
IT UNFOLDS EVERY HOUR.
A SOFT WORD SPOKE.
HERE AND THERE.
A KISS GIVEN UNAWARE.
A GENTLE TOUCH CAN
MEAN SO MUCH IN
MAKING LOVE AND THAT
FLOWER GROW.
TAKE THE TIME AND LET
THAT SPECIAL SOMEONE
KNOW.
"DARLING. I LOVE YOU SO."

LDM

1/30/1995
11:35 A.M.

## BROKEN HEART

YOU TOOK MY HEART
AND BROKE IT.
WHAT A HURTING
SOUND. I CAN FEEL
THE PIECES LYING
AROUND.
WOULD IT HAVE
BEEN SAFER IF I HAD
PLACED IT ON A
SHELF?
OR
PERHAPS BETTER
PROTECTED GIVEN TO
SOMEONE ELSE?
I LOOK IN VARIOUS
PLACES FOR THE
MISSING PARTS TO
MEND MY BROKEN
HEART.
WHEN THE SEARCH
HAS ENDED AND I
FIND MY BROKEN
HEART IS MENDED.
BUT
WHAT ABOUT MY
MIND?

LDM

02/07/1995
3:50 P.M.

## SOMEONE

I NEED SOMEONE TO HOLD ME WHEN I
CRY. I NEED SOMEONE TO HOLD ME
WHEN I CRY.
AS THE TEARS WELL UP INSIDE. I NEED
SOMEONE TO HOLD ME WHEN I CRY.
WHEN THE TEARS FALL FROM MY EYES.
I NEED SOMEONE TO HOLD ME WHEN I
CRY.
OFTENTIMES THE WORLD SEEMS SO
COLD AND DAILY CARES SEEM TO
TOUCH MY SOUL. I NEED SOMEONE TO
HOLD ME WHEN I CRY.
WHEN MY HEART SEEMS TO BREAK IN
TWO AND I REACH OUT FOR YOU. I NEED
SOMEONE TO HOLD ME WHEN I CRY.


LDM

# A PLAYERS PLEA

ON THAT DAY WHEN I WENT
OUT TO PLAY. I NEVER
MEANT TO GIVE MY HEART
AWAY.
I ONLY WENT OUT FOR A
LITTLE WHILE. I WAS
CAPTIVATED BY YOUR
SMILE.
I DIDNT MEAN TO STAY. I
JUST WANTED TO PLAY.
OH WHY DID I CHOOSE THAT
DAY?
WHY DID I GO THERE TO
PLAY?
OH WHY OH WHY. DID I GIVE
MY HEART AWAY?

NOW I WANT YOU TO GIVE
MY HEART BACK TO ME.
BUT I KNOW THAT CAN
NEVER BE.
FOR WHEN I SEE YOUR
SMILE. ALL THE PAIN IS
WORTHWHILE.
BUT YET I SAY. WHY DID I
GIVE MY HEART AWAY?

LDM

10/13/1998

# U-TURN

IN THE VACANT PLACES OF MY MIND. I
CAN ALWAYS FIND U.
U-TURN MY NIGHTMARES INTO DREAMS
U-TURN MY TEARS INTO SCREAMS OF
ECSTASY_SOMETIMES
U-TURN JOY INTO SORROW
U-TURN YESTERDAY INTO HOPE FOR
TOMORROW
U- TURN ME ON
IN THE VACANT PLACES OF MY MIND
I CAN ALWAYS FIND U.

LDM

# <u>LOOKING</u>

TEMPTING. TANTALIZING
WARM. CARAMEL. SWEET
FROM THE TOP OF YOUR HEAD
TO THE SOLES OF YOUR FEET.

HEART GOING PUTTER PATTER
WHEN YOU ARE AROUND
I HEAR ONLY YOUR VOICE
NO OTHER SOUND.

LOOK AT YOU. LOOK AT YOU
AS YOU GO STROLLING BY
MY OH MY! HOW I
WISH YOU WERE MINE.

SO FINE. SO FINE
MOUTHWATERING KIND.
WARM. CARAMEL SWEET
FROM THE TOP OF YOUR HEAD
TO THE SOLES OF YOUR FEET

LDM.
06/11/2001

# A ROSE 🌹 BEHIND THE WALL

I LOOK IN YOUR SAD FACE.
A MOUTH WITHOUT A
SMILE
YOU ARE SO TIMID
LIKE A FRIGHTENED CHILD.
WHEN I COME CLOSE.
YOU WITHDRAW
AS IF THERE IS A WARNING
THERE.
CAN'T YOU TELL BY MY
ACTION THAT I TRULY
CARE?
YOUR THORNS ARE SHARP.
HOW DARE I BE PRICKED.
ADVANCES TO YOU MUST
BE QUIET AND QUICK.
WHY ARE YOU SO
GUARDED?
EACH DAY MORE IN LOVE I
FALL.
COME OUT INTO THE
GARDEN STOP HIDING A
ROSE BEHIND THE WALL.

LDM

7/25/95
3:40 PM

# BLENDING

GREEN EYES,
GOLDEN BLONDE MINGLED WITH
GREY HAIR.
A STRONG SMILE. A HEART THAT CARES.
A SOUL THAT I CAN TOUCH, YOU ARE SUCH A
MIND- BENDING PERSON.
RACE MEANING THE COLORING
DOES NOT AFFECT THE TIME OR THE
PLEASURE.
WE FIND RACE MEANING THE. IT DOES NOT
MEASURE THE LOVE THAT'S SHARED BY YOU
AND I.


LDM

# BEAUTY

OH YOU BROWN EYED BEAUTY.
WITH THE CHOCOLATE SKIN.
WHAT HAUNTING SECRETS DO YOU HOLD WITHIN?

YOU BROWN EYED BEAUTY
WITH THAT CHOCOLATE SKIN
HOW I DESIRE YOU. IS THAT A SIN?

MY. MY BROWN EYED BEAUTY
DELICIOUS CHOCOLATE SKIN. TAKE A CHANCE ON ME
AND LET ME IN.

I WILL TREAT YOU WITH LOVING CARE. MY HEART
WITH YOU ONLY WILL I SHARE.

BROWN EYED BEAUTY WITH CHOCOLATE SKIN.
NOW IS YOUR CHANCE LET ME IN.
OH HOW I DESIRE YOU. IS THAT A SIN?
BROWN EYED BEAUTY WITH THE CHOCOLATE SKIN.

LDM

# A VALENTINE FOR MY VALENTIME

MY VALENTINE IS KINDA FADED.
HE HAS FURROWS IN HIS BROW.
I DIDN'T LOVE MY VALENTINE THEN
AS MUCH AS I DO NOW.
HE IS SOMEWHAT WRINKLED AND
HIS HAIR IS TURNING GRAY.
I WILL ALWAYS LOVE MY
VALENTINE COME WHAT MAY.
OUR LOVE HAS WEATHERED THE
STORM. WE DID NOT DRIFT APART.
WE HAVE BEEN EACH OTHERS
ANCHOR BECAUSE WE ARE HELD
HEART TO HEART.
THE KISSES WE SHARE ARE JUST
AS FIERY AS THEY WERE LONG
AGO.
EACH YEAR I FIND I LOVE MY
VALENTIME SO. SO. SO MUCH MORE

LDM.

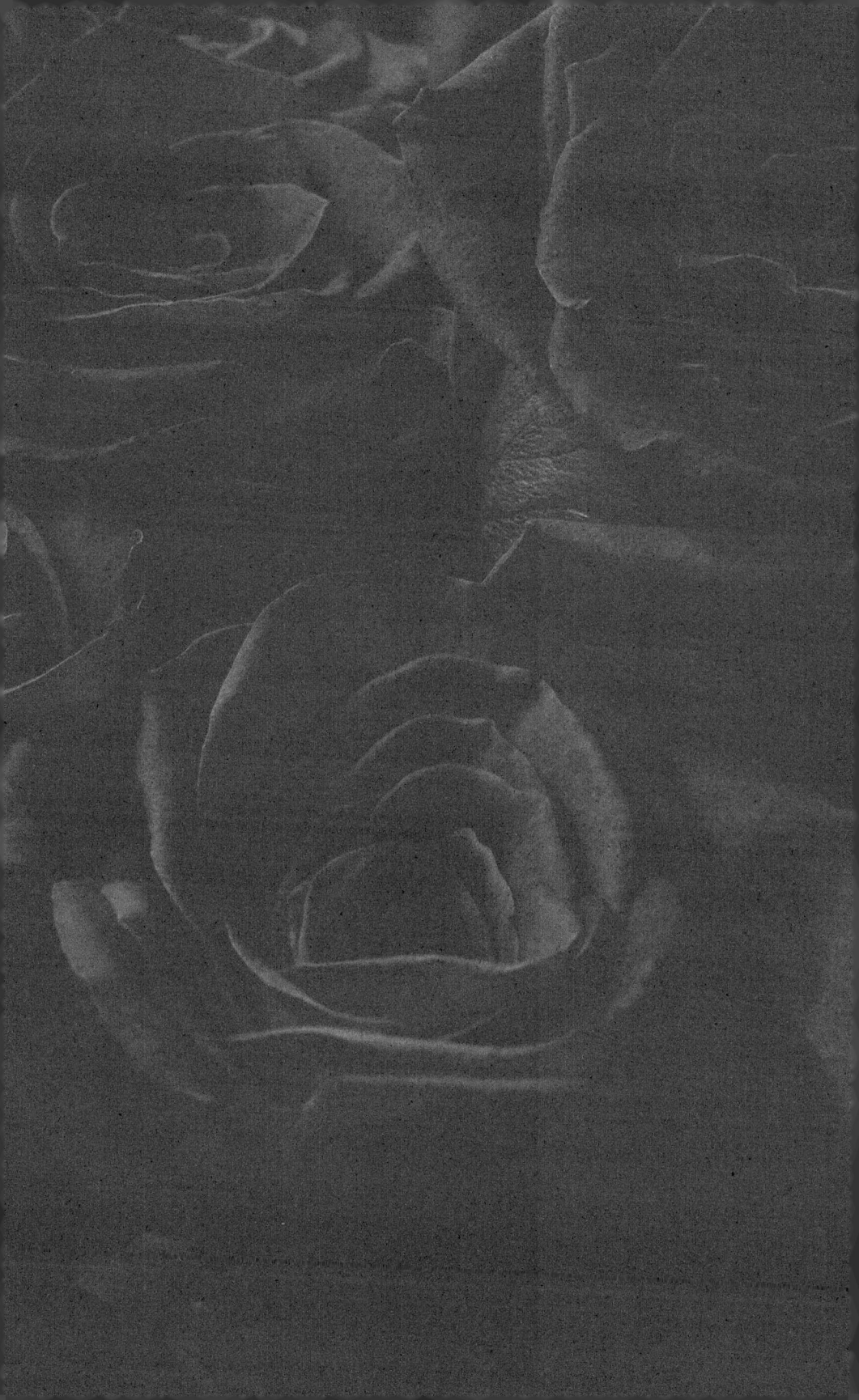

# SWEET SWEET YOU

YOUR WARM BROWN SKIN IS LIKE MY
SATURDAY MORNING TOAST
THAT I SPREAD MY STRAWBERRY JAM
ON WHICH SATISFIES MY TASTE BUDS
AS YOUR SOFT VOICE FLOWING FROM
THOSE SENSUOUS FULL DARK LIPS.
WARMS MY MIND AS THIS CUP OF MILD
COFFEE STIMULATES THE ADRENALINE IN
MY BODY. SWEET SWEET YOU.

A SMILE THAT MAKES THE SUNSHINE
LOSE ITS GLOW AND RAINBOWS
APPEAR AS DAFFODILS.
SUNFLOWERS. ROSES. CARNATIONS TAKE
ON A NEW FRAGRANCE ALL BECAUSE OF
YOUR SMILE.

YOUR TOUCH CAN MAKE TIME STAND
STILL AS MY SENSES COME ALIVE. MY
MIND RECONNECTING ITSELF TO MY BODY.
YOUR PRESENCE IS LIKE BEING BUNDLED
UP IN GRANDMOTHERS OLD QUILT IN
FRONT OF A FIREPLACE HEARING THE
RAINDROPS AS THEY FALL SOFTLY ON
THE ROOFTOP.

SWEET SWEET YOU.
YOUR KINDNESS. CARING. GENTLENESS IS
LIKE BEING BACK IN MY MOTHER'S WOMB
BEING GIVEN ALL THE THINGS THAT
MAKE ME FEEL SAFE. SECURE AND
LOVED.
SWEET SWEET YOU

LDM

# BOUNDARIES

WARM BROWN CHOCOLATE SKIN
EBONY EYES. BIG WIDE GRIN.
STRONG ARMS AND CALLOUSED HANDS.
A VOICE SO TENDER. A HEART THAT UNDERSTANDS.
THOSE SEEM TO BE A FEW OF THE THINGS THAT MAKE YOU
ATTRACTIVE TO ME
BUT YOU ARE BOUND BY THE CORDS OF TIME.
YOU CANT SEEM TO UNWIND
AND SET YOURSELF FREE
SO I CAN SEE JUST WHAT IS THERE
THAT MAYBE I CAN REPAIR.
WITHIN THAT WARM BROWN CHOCOLATE SKIN.
EBONY EYES. BIG WIDE GRIN.
EMANCIPATE YOUR SOUL.
UNLEASH SELF- CONTROL.
LIFE WASNT MEANT TO LIVE SO CAUTIOUSLY
FILL IT WITH ECSTASY.
COME FROM WITHIN THAT SHELL OF WARM BROWN CHOCOLATE
SKIN.
BRIGHTEN THOSE EBONY EYES. SOFTEN THAT BIG WIDE GRIN.
WARM BROWN CHOCOLATE SKIN.


LDM

# MY IVORY PRINCE

LOOK AT THEM HOW THEY STARE.
THEY DON'T UNDERSTAND THE LOVE WE
SHARE.
I FIND IT SO EASY TO CARE FOR YOU
MY IVORY PRINCE.
WITH YOUR LONG, LUSCIOUS AND ALL SO
SENSUOUS WHITE FRAME
YOU CAME INTO MY CINNAMON
SPRINKLED WORLD. YOU MADE ME FEEL
LIKE A BRONZED GIRL.
YOU SPOKE AND YOUR VOICE SOUNDED
LIKE MUSIC TO MY EAR. IT WAS JUST
WHAT I NEEDED TO HEAR.
THERE WASN'T A COMMUNICATION GAP
WITH YOUR SWEET SOUTHERN DRAWL. I
CAN'T RECALL JUST WHAT WAS SAID
THAT TURNED MY HEAD.
RIGHT FROM THE START. YOU STOLE MY
HEART.
THEY DON'T SEEM TO UNDERSTAND LOVE
IS NOT THE COLOR OF MAN. IT SPRINGS
FROM SOMEWHERE WITHIN A PLACE
THEY HAVE NEVER BEEN.
LET THEM STARE. THEY WILL NEVER
UNDERSTAND THE LOVE WE SHARE.
THEY WILL ALWAYS LIVE APART
BECAUSE TO TRULY LOVE YOU MUST
HAVE A HEART.

LDM

6/3/99

# COLOR LINES

WHITE AS WHITE
ON A SNOW COVERED HILL
BLACK AS MIDNIGHT
SO QUIET, SO STILL
YOU AND I
MY LIPS ON YOURS
YOUR LIPS ON MINE

LEGS, ARMS ENTWINED
HEARTS BEATING A RHYME

YOU INSIDE ME
ME ENCLOSING YOU
BECOMING ONE
OUR BODIES MOVE IN PERFECT MOTION
AND THE FUELS OF ECSTASY EXPLODE

YOUR SWEAT AND MINE TASTE THE
SAME
WHERE IS THE COLOR LINE?
WE CLOSE OUR EYES
YOURS SKY BLUE, MINE HAZELNUT
BROWN
AND SURRENDER TO A LOVE RAPTURED
SLEEP STILL ENTWINED
WHERE IS THE COLOR LINE?

LDM
06/13/2001
9:15 AM

29

# DARK & SWEET

BLACKER THAN ANYTHING I'VE EVER SEEN
UNLESS IT WAS IN A MIDNIGHT DREAM

_YOU

SWEETER THAN HONEY AND CREAM
_YOU

A SMILE THAT CAN LIFT UP THE DARK EYES
SO DREAMY THEY ALONE CAN BREAK A HEART
_YOU

A TOUCH THAT MAKES ME FEEL COMPLETE

_YOU

DARK SWEET
DARK SWEET
DARK SWEET
_YOU

LDM

THIS POETIC EXPRESSION IS DEDICATED TO ALL
THE WOMEN THAT LIKE THEIR MAN
"SPECIALLY DARK"
BUT AS FOR ME
PUT A LOTTA CREAM IN MINE

# CALL ME "BABY"

HOW CASUAL THAT WORD IS WHEN
YOU HEAR IT. BUT WHEN IT'S REALLY
SAID TO YOU THE SOFTNESS. THE
PROTECTION. THE VULNERABILITY
CAUSES YOU TO MELT INSIDE.

YOUR KNEES BECOME WEAK. YOUR
BRAIN SIZZLES. YOUR TONGUE GETS
LOUD AND SOUL EXPLODES.

YOUR DEFENSES ARE NO LONGER
WORTH DEFENDING AND YOUR
BROKEN HEART IS MENDED.

WHEN YOU CALL ME "BABY" I'M
YOURS.

LDM

3/25/03

# MY LIFETIME FRIEND

IN YOUR EYES I YET SEE THE SPECIAL
SPARK THATS ONLY FOR ME
YOUR FACE IS OLDER NOW AND FULL OF
LINES, AN INDICATION OF A CHARACTER
THAT CAN ONLY COME WITH TIME

YOUR LIPS ARE YET FULL ABOVE A VERY
FIRM CHIN, A SMILE THAT OFTEN TURNS
INTO AN IMPISH GRIN

YOU ARE STILL IN MY HEART A FINE YOUNG
MAN YEARS HAVE GIVEN ME TO
UNDERSTAND, YOUR PHYSICAL FEATURES
ARE NICE THATS TRUE BUT THATS NOT THE
REASON I CHOSE YOU TO BE MY LIFETIME
FRIEND

THE PART OF YOU THE EYES CAN NEVER
SEE IS WHAT MEANS SO MUCH TO ME
YOUR HEART OF GOLD
YOUR SELF CONTROL
YOUR LOVING TOUCH
THAT MEANS SO MUCH
YOU SO UNSELFISHLY GAVE TO ME THOSE
THINGS YOU POSSESS WITHIN
THATS WHY I CHOSE YOU TO BE MY
LIFETIME FRIEND

LDM

32

# TODAY I BECAME A WOMAN

I LAY HERE IN YOUR ARMS AFTER
I'VE GIVEN MYSELF TO YOU
I FEEL A GLOW INSIDE AS IF I HAD
BEEN WASHED WITH THE MORNING
DEW
I FEEL YOUR HEARTBEAT.
I CAN EVEN HEAR THE SOUND
I SAY WITHIN MYSELF
HAPPINESS I'VE TRULY FOUND
YESTERDAY I WAS A GIRL
ONE BY MYSELF
NOW I AM APART OF SOMEONE ELSE
MY THOUGHTS HAVE BEEN
TRANSFORMED
I FEEL WHOLE COMPLETE
SO NEW. YES SO YOUNG
TODAY I BECAME A WOMAN


LDM

# UNTITLED

THE TIME WE SPENT TOGETHER
WAS JUST TO EASE OUR LONELINESS
TWO PEOPLE SEARCHING FOR THAT
SOMETHING
REACHING OUT TRYING TO FILL AN
EMPTY PLACE
NOT THINKING ABOUT TOMORROW OR
ANYTHING FOR THE FUTURE
ALL I ASK IS THAT YOU HOLD ME
LIKE I AM YOUR ONE TRUE LOVE

WE ARE TOUCHING PLACES THAT
HAVE NOT BEEN TOUCHED IN AWHILE
HOLDING ON TO ONE ANOTHER WITH
NO THOUGHTS OF TOMORROW
TRYING NOT TO THINK OF WHAT
MIGHT COULD BE
REACHING THOSE HEIGHTS OF
ECSTASY
WE ARE HOLDING ONE ANOTHER LIKE
WE ARE OUR ONE TRUE LOVE
WHEN DAYLIGHT COME WE WILL
WALK AWAY. THINKING BUT NOT
HAVING MUCH TO SAY.

TODAY IS THAT TOMORROW
YET WE WANTED TO HOLD ONE
ANOTHER AS IF WE WERE THAT ONE
TRUE LOVE
OH SO TONIGHT WE MEET AGAIN
THIS SEEMINGLY IS BECOMING A
REGULAR THING
SOON IT WILL BE COMMON. SOON IT
WILL BE TOO COMMON AND THE
TIME WE SPEND TOGETHER WILL NOT
BE TO EASE OUR LONELINESS IT WILL
BECOME A TIME OF WANTING TO BE
APART
WE WILL END UP WITH BROKEN
HEARTS
SO LETS WALK AWAY BEFORE WE
HAVE HURTING WORDS TO SAY......
AND WE WILL NO LONGER WANT TO
HOLD EACH OTHER AS OUR OWN ONE
TRUE LOVE
LETS LET IT BE
YOU STAY WITH YOU AND ILL STAY
WITH ME

LDM
12/14/15

# <u>TWO BECOMES ONE</u>

THE NIGHT I MADE YOU MINE MY
DARLING DEAR ONLY OUR HEART
BEATS WERE HEARD
WE HAD NO SENSE OF TIME THERE
WAS NO SPOKEN WORD
I PLACED A KISS ON YOUR BROW
I HEARD YOUR INVITING SIGHS
I HELD YOUR FACE IN MY HANDS AS
I LOOKED INTO YOUR EYES
YOU WERE SO WARM YOUR TOUCH
SO SOFT AND GENTLE
THE LIGHT ON YOUR FACE I WILL
ALWAYS REMEMBER
I TOUCHED YOUR LIPS WITH MY
TONGUE AND TASTED YOUR VERY
SOUL
THE FIRE THAT WAS IGNITED WILL
NEVER GO COLD
YOU CAME TO ME WITH
RESERVATIONS NONE
ON THAT NIGHT MY DARLING DEAR
TWO BECAME ONE

LDM
95

# MY BREAST

TAUNTLY, TIGHTLY AND TANTALIZING
THEY FORM BEAUTIFUL MOUNDS
UPON MY CHEST
WITH THE NOURISHMENT OF LIFE IN
A MILKY FLUID THAT FLOWS FROM
MY BREAST

WHEN SOME CHILD IS LONELY OR
WHEN SLEEP FILLS THEIR EYES AND
THEY NEED TO REST
THEY CURL THEIR LITTLE ARMS
AROUND MY NECK AND REST THEIR
HEADS ON MY BREAST

WHEN MY LOVER COMES TO ME AND
CARESSES ME TENDERLY, I FEEL THE
STRENGTH OF HIS CHEST A YEARNING
HE AWAKENS FLOWS INTO MY
BREAST

MY LOVER FEELS THE NEED IN ME
AND KISSES THEM PASSIONATELY
AND HE KNOWS IN A MOMENT HE
HAS AROSE A DESIRE IN ME I MUST
CONFESS
THE KEY TO MY EROTIC SOUL LIES
WITHIN MY BREAST


LDM

# STRANGE FLESH

IS IN MY SENSES
LOOK AT YOU
TOUCH YOU
HOLD YOU
KISS AND CARESS YOU
TO ALLOW MYSELF TO BE ENGULFED
BY YOU
I NEVER SHOULD HAVE TASTED YOUR
STRANGE FLESH

NOW THE SCENT IS IN MY SENSES
MY EYES LOOK FOR YOU
MY HANDS LONG TO TOUCH YOU
MY ARMS ACHE TO HOLD YOU
MY LIPS MY TONGUE WANTS TO
KISS YOU
MY FINGERS WANT TO CARESS YOU
MY MOST PRIVATE BEING THATS
UNITED WITH SOMEONE ELSE
WANTS TO BE ENGULFED IN YOUR
STRANGE FLESH

LDM

# POWER OF THE P'NIS

THROBBING AND THRUSTING THIS
MIGHTY THING
IT IS POSSESSED BY PAUPAS AND
KINGS
IT HAS CAUSED MANY A BATTLE TO
BE FOUGHT
FROM BOARD TO BEDROOM IT HAS
BEEN SOUGHT
THE MEASURE OF ITS POWER OR
THE MIGHT OF ITS STRENGTH
CANNOT BE EXPRESSED IN ITS SIZE
THE PENIS HAS A POWER OF ITS
OWN YOU MUST REALIZE
FROM IT LIFE IS PLANTED TO GROW
ENDLESSLY
YOU MUST KNOW HOW TO HARNESS
THAT POWER FOR A WORLD OF
TROUBLE CAN ERUPT
YOU CANNOT STRIKE EVERY TIME
AND PLACE IT RISES UP
YOU MUST HAVE THE SENSE OF
CONTROL
LISTEN TO WHAT YOU ARE BEING
TOLD
IT WILL RUN YOU DOWN WHILE YOU
ARE YOUNG
YOU ALSO WANT TO USE ITS POWER
WHEN YOU ARE OLD
WHETHER YOU ARE ON EARTH, MARS
OR VENUS
USE IT WISELY AND THERE WILL
ALWAYS BE POWER IN THE PENIS

LDM

# CRY BETWEEN MY THIGH

THE CRY BETWEEN MY THIGHS SEEM
TO IGNITE MY WHOLE BODY
SENDING AN EXPLOSION INTO THE
BRAIN. THE SOUL. THE HEART
THAT EXPLOSION SEEMS TO ENGULF
THE ENTIRE NERVOUS SYSTEM
IT LUBRICATES THE THOUGHT
PATTERN. THE MIND EXPLODES AND
TEARS YOUR ENTIRE BEING APART
YET YOUR EXTERIOR SELF HAS TO
STAY INTACT. YOU HAVE TO APPEAR
AS IF NOTHING SO DRASTIC IS
OCCURING INTERNALLY
FOR THE LACK OF SOMEONE TO
EXTINGUISH THAT FIRE
YOUR EYES MUST CRY INTERNAL
TEARS
AS THE HEAT INTENSIFIES. YOUR
EXTERIOR SELF MUST REMAIN
INTACT
HOPEFULLY THE FIRE WILL NOT
CAUSE YOU TO CRY OUT AUDIBLY TO
SOME LOST LOVE OR A LOVER THAT
TOOK THE CRYING BETWEEN YOUR
THIGHS IN YOUR YOUTH. BETRAYED
YOU. LEAVING LONELY FLESHLY
BEINGS RESEMBLING THE BOTH OF
YOU

QUESTIONS THAT YOU NOW PONDER
IN YOUR MIND AS TO WHY A GOD
THAT LOVES. PROVIDES. PROTECTS
AND RESTORES YOU. SEEMINGLY HAS
LEFT YOU WITH THIS INFERNO.
MAYBE THE GOD WHO IS
OMNIPRESENT IS JEALOUS BEACUSE I
HAVE NOT LEARNED TO LOVE HIM
THE GREAT I AM THAT DOES
EVERYTHING FOR ME INCLUDING
SUFFERING ALONG WITH ME WHILE
THIS CRY BETWEEN MY THIGHS
BURNS LIKE AN INFERNO
HE WILL NOT ALLOW MY SOUL TO
BE CONSUMED BY THAT FIRE. IF ILL
ONLY TRUST HIM
THE CRIES BETWEEN MY THIGHS CAN
BE FELT ALL THROUGH THE NIGHT
OFTENTIMES THE MOURNFUL SOUNDS
RESONATE DURING THE DAYLIGHT


LDM

# UNTITLED

YOUR SEED IS PLANTED IN THIS
FERTILE GROUND
WHEN THE FRUIT COMES FORTH
WILL IT BE WHITE OR BROWN?

THE LOVE THAT WE SHARE TO
MAKE THIS PERFECT BEING
COULD WELL COME FORTH WITH
ROYALTY AS A KING

I KNOW THIS CHILD WILL BE
SPECIAL. IT WILL HAVE THE BEST OF
BOTH OF US
WITH LOVE THAT KNOWS NO
BOUNDARIES
WHICH CAN ONLY BE A PLUS

WITH A HEART OF PURE GOLD
UNITY HE WILL HOLD
HE WILL NOT BE SUPERFICIAL
BUT WILL BE A COMPASSIONATE
SOUL

THIS SEED OF KINDNESS. PEACE. UNITY
THIS SEED FROM YOU AND ME
THIS WARM TAN BLUE EYED BUNDLE
OF LOVE


LDM

## LOVE

A PAIN THAT PIERCES THE SOUL
CAUSES THE HEART TO BLEED AS
TEARS FALL FROM YOUR EYES
WHILE YOUR LIPS SMILE
LOVE
LOVE THE ULTIMATE JOY IN PAIN
ONE OF THE STRONGEST EMOTIONS
ALONG WITH THE FRATERNAL
TWIN EMOTION HATE
THAT THIN LINE IS EVER PRESENT
THAT SEPARATES THE TWO
EMOTIONS

LDM

# CHEATED AND CHEATER

I HAD A ONE NIGHT STAND A LONG
TIME AGO
ALL I WAS DOING WAS TRYING TO
EVEN THE SCORE
I GOT WHERE I ENJOYED IT AND I
WENT BACK ONCE MORE
THE GRASS WAS GREENER AND THE
WATER WAS SWEETER I THOUGHT
SQUEEZING AND TEASING LOOK
WHAT I BROUGHT
WRECKED LINES LOST
COMMUNICATION TIME SPENT IN
VAIN
I DIDNT COUNT UP THE COST BEFORE
I PLAYED THE CHEATING GAME
NOW IM IN AND OUT OF
RELATIONSHIPS WITH SO MANY
LOVERS
I CHEAT ON ONE WITH THE OTHER
ITS BECOME A JUGGLING ACT
AS EACH LIFE I TOSS
IVE LOST ALL SENSE OF
COMMITMENT
NOTHING COULD BE NEATER
A LONG TIME I LOST
NOW I HAVE THE LIFE OF A
CHEATER

LDM

# <u>STAY</u>

DONT RUN AWAY PLEASE STAY.
LETS FIND OUT WHAT ITS ALL
ABOUT. DONT RUN AWAY PLEASE
STAY
WE HAD A FIGHT THE OTHER NIGHT
OVER SOME SILLY THING. YOU GOT
MAD AND GAVE ME BACK MY RING
DONT RUN AWAY PLEASE STAY.
LETS FIND OUT WHAT ITS ALL
ABOUT
I WILL LOVE YOU FOR THE REST OF
MY LIFE I WANT YOU TO BE MY
WIFE
DONT RUN AWAY PLEASE STAY.
LETS FIND OUT WHAT ITS ALL
ABOUT
I KNOW I WAS WRONG WHEN I
STAYED OUT ALL NIGHT LONG
I NEEDED SOME TIME TO MYSELF
ITS YOU I LOVE THERE IS NO ONE
ELSE
GIRL. YOU MUST UNDERSTAND
I AM A COMPLEX MAN
YOU MEAN THE WORLD TO ME
DONT WALK OUT THE DOOR
YOURE HURTING ME SO. SO. SO
DONT RUN AWAY PLEASE STAY

LETS FIND OUT WHAT ITS ALL
ABOUT
IM BEGGING YOU BABY
DONT RUN AWAY. PLEASE STAY
LETS FIND OUT WHAT ITS ALL
ABOUT
IM ON BENDING KNEES LISTEN. LISTEN.
LISTEN TO ME
DONT RUN AWAY. PLEASE STAY.
LETS FIND OUT WHAT ITS ALL
ABOUT
PLEASE. PLEASE. PLEASE
DONT RUN AWAY. BABY STAY. BABY
STAY
LET US FIND OUT WHAT ITS ALL
ABOUT
DONT RUN AWAY. PLEASE STAY.
DONT RUN AWAY. PLEASE STAY

SOMEBODY SOMWEHERE IS GOING THROUGH
THIS IT FELL IN SPIRIT ON THE EVENING OF
GOOD FRIDAY 2004 I HOPE SOMEDAY IT
WILL BE A BLESSING TO WHO EVER NEEDS
A WORD

LDM
4/9/2004
512 PM

# PROMISES & LOVE

SOMEBODY BREAKS A PROMISE
SOMEBODY BREAKS A HEART
LOVE CAN TEAR YOU APART

WHAT DO YOU WANT FROM A
FATHER?
WHAT DO YOU WANT FROM A
BROTHER?
WHAT DO YOU WANT FROM A
SISTER?
WHAT DO YOU WANT FROM A
MOTHER?
WHAT DO YOU WANT FROM A
FRIEND?
WHAT DO YOU WANT FROM A
LOVER?

PROMISES ARE SOMETIMES NEVER
REMEMBERED
THEY GIVE AND TAKE UNTIL THEY
FALL APART
A PROMISE CAN BREAK A STRONG
MANS HEART
PROMISES ARENT EASY TO KEEP OR
BREAK ITS GIVE OR TAKE

WHAT DO YOU WANT FROM A
FATHER?
WHAT DO YOU WANT FROM A
BROTHER?
WHAT DO YOU WANT FROM A
SISTER?
WHAT DO YOU WANT FROM A
MOTHER?
WHAT DO YOU WANT FROM A
FRIEND?
WHAT DO YOU WANT FROM A
LOVER?

SOMEBODY BREAKS A PROMISE
SOMEBODY BREAKS A HEART
LOVE CAN TEAR A STRONG MAN
APART

YES PROMISES & LOVE CAN TEAR
YOU APART

LDM

# STEADFAST

I FELT YOU SLIPPING AWAY
THERE WAS NOTHING I COULD DO
OR SAY
MY HAND WAS THERE FOR YOU
TO HOLD
MY VOICE TO COMFORT AND
CONSOLE YET I FELT YOU SLIPPING
AWAY

YOURE MY STRENGTH
YOURE MY WEAKNESS
YOURE THE BETTER PART OF ME
MY MIND COULD NOT CONCEIVE
WHAT MY EYES SAW
WHAT MY HEART WOULD NOT
BELIEVE I FELT YOU SLIPPING
AWAY

FIGHT MY LOVE YOU MUST LIVE
TO EACH OTHER WE HAVE SO
MUCH TO GIVE
MANKIND WOULD SUFFER A
TERRIBLE LOSS
WE MUST WIN THIS BATTLE AT
ALL COST
IM HOLDING YOU MUST STAY
I WILL NOT LET YOU SLIP AWAY

THE SUN SHONE BRIGHT THROUGH
THE DARK DARK NIGHT
I BELIEVE WE'VE LEARNED TO
FIGHT
WE HOLD ON THROUGH IT ALL
SURVIVED THE PAIN FROM THE
FALL
IM HOLDING YOU MUST STAY
I WILL NOT LET YOU SLIP AWAY


LDM

# COMPROMISE

YOU WALKED INTO MY LIFE AT A
SPECIAL TIME LEAVING YOUR
FOOTPRINTS ON MY MIND
THERE IS SOMEPLACE ELSE YOU
HAVE TO BE IT DOESNT
MEAN
YOU DONT LOVE ME
I WANTED YOU
SHE NEEDS YOU
THERE IS SOMEPLACE ELSE YOU
HAVE TO BE IT DOESNT MEAN YOU
DONT LOVE ME
THE SUNLIGHT FILTERS THROUGH
MY WINDOW SHADE
SHINING ON THE PLACE WHERE
YOUR HEAD LAID
LAST NIGHT AS WE HELD EACH
OTHER TIGHT FEELING OUR
HEARTS BEAT AS ONE
AS THEY HAVE DONE SO MANY
TIMES BEFORE
THERE WILL ALWAYS BE AN OPEN
DOOR HERE FOR YOU MY LOVE
I WANT YOU
SHE NEEDS YOU
THERE IS SOMEPLACE ELSE YOU
HAVE TO BE IT DOESNT MEAN YOU
DONT LOVE ME

THE CLOCK TICKS SO SLOWLY AS I
WAIT FOR YOU
I UNDERSTAND YOU HAVE OTHER
THINGS TO DO
EACH TIME YOU RETURN I WILL
BE HERE CHERISHING EVERY
MOMENT YOU ARE NEAR
YOU WALKED INTO MY LIFE AT A
SPECIAL TIME LEAVING YOUR
FOOTPRINTS ON MY MIND
I WANT YOU
SHE NEEDS YOU
THERE IS SOMEPLACE ELSE YOU
HAVE TO BE. IT DOESN'T MEAN
YOU DONT LOVE ME
WHAT WE HAVE IS ALL SO TRUE
SO I DO WHAT I MUST DO
I PLACE YOU IN MY HEART. WE
ARE NEVER APART
I WANT YOU
SHE NEEDS YOU
THERE IS SOMEPLACE YOU HAVE
TO BE. IT DOESNT MEAN YOU DONT
LOVE ME
I WILL ALWAYS WAIT. NO IM NOT
CHEATING THE HAND OF FATE
YOU ARE NEVER TOO LATE
I WANT YOU
SHE NEEDS YOU
THERE IS SOMEPLACE YOU HAVE
TO BE. IT DOESNT MEAN YOU DONT
LOVE ME

LDM

## AMEND

WHAT AM I GOING TO DO IF YOU
DONT COME HOME IN THE
MORNING?
WHAT WILL I TELL OUR SON
WHEN HE ASKS FOR HIS MOM?
WHAT AM I GOING TO DO IF YOU
DONT COME HOME IN THE
MORNING?
WHEN OUR LITTLE GIRL CRIES
CAUSE HER HAIR WONT CURL
AND KEEPS FALLING IN HER EYES
WHAT WILL I DO IF YOU DONT
COME HOME IN THE MORNING?
THE CEREAL IS GONE. THE MILK IS
TOO. NO ONE CAN MAKE PANCAKES
LIKE YOU DO
WHAT AM I GOING TO DO IF YOU
DONT COME HOME IN THE
MORNING?

HOW WILL I TIE MY TIE OR
STRAIGHTEN MY COLLAR?
WHO WILL I KISS BYE BYE IF YOU
DONT COME HOME IN THE
MORNING?
THESE ROSES WILL WILT. THESE
CANDLES WILL BURN OUT. THE
WINE WILL BE FLAT
THE DISAGREEMENT WASNT A
MAJOR CRISIS
IT WAS JUST A LOVERS SPAT
YOU DIDNT HAVE TO WALK OUT
LIKE THAT
WHAT AM I GOING TO DO IF YOU
DONT COME HOME IN TJHE
MORNING?
YOU ARE SPECIAL TO ME DEAR. I
WISH YOU WERE HERE
I KNOW YOU CARE. THE WAY I
NEGLECTED YOU WASNT FAIR
WHAT WILL I DO IF YOU DONT
COME HOME IN THE MORNING?


LDM
05/15/2003

# NOW AND THEN

MY DEAR WILL YOU STILL LOVE
ME WHEN I HAVE GROWN OLD
WHEN THE HAND ONCE SO SOFT
TO TOUCH IS NOW DRY AND COLD

MY DEAR WILL YOU STILL LOVE
ME WHEN I BECOME AS A CHILD
AND ALL I CAN DO IS LOOK AT
YOU AND SMILE

MY DEAR WILL YOU STILL LOVE
ME WHEN MY HAIR TURNS GRAY
THE DAYS OF MY BEAUTY SEEM
TO HAVE SLIPPED AWAY

MY DEAR WILL YOU STILL LOVE
ME WHEN I CAN NO LONGER WALK
WHEN MY CONVERSATION IS A
RAMBLED TALK

MY DEAR WILL YOU STILL LOVE
ME
WHEN YOU CAN ONLY SIT AT MY
BEDSIDE AND THINK OF WHAT
USED TO BE WITH TEAR FILLED
EYES.

MY DEAR WILL YOU STILL LOVE
ME WHEN MY EYES ARE CLOSED
IN DEATH OR WILL YOU HAVE
LEFT ME LONG AGO FOR SOMEONE
ELSE

MY DEAR AS YOU PLEDGE YOUR
LOVE FOR ME ON THIS SPECIAL
DAY
YOU ARE SAYING YOU WILL LOVE
ME COME WHAT MAY

MY DEAR LOVE IS NOT JUST THE
PASSION THAT BURNS SO WITHIN
LOVE IS THE TEST OF TIME AND
ITS WHAT MAKES US FRIENDS

MY DEAR DO YOU LOVE ME?

LDM

# TEACH ME

TEACH ME TO LOVE WITHOUT
CONDITIONS.
TO LOVE WITH A LOVE THAT IS
PURE WITH NO GREAT
EXPECTATIONS.
TEACH ME TO LOVE IF NO LOVE IS
GIVEN IN RETURN.
TEACH ME TO LOVE SO THERE
WILL BE THE BLENDING OF SKIN SO
I CAN ONLY SEE THE RED COLOR
OF BLOOD THAT FLOWS IN THE
VEINS OF MY FELLOWMAN.
THAT BLOOD THAT WARMS THE
HEART AND CAUSES THE HEART
TO OVERFLOW INTO MY EYES AND
I CAN ONLY SEE MY FACE IN THE
FACE OF MY FELLOWMAN AND
KNOW THAT HE IS PART OF ME.

TEACH ME TO LOVE BEYOND
TRUST
TEACH ME TO LOVE WITHOUT
FEAR
TEACH ME TO KNOW AND LOVE
MYSELF SO I CAN COMPLETELY
LOVE OTHERS.

LDM

## THE WAY WE ARE

YOUNG. PASSIONATE. HARD TO
HOLD. BODIES ON FIRE. JUST OUT
OF CONTROL
HANDS TOUCHING. TONGUES
EXPLORING. HEARTS BEATING WILD.
EYES SEARCHING TO SEE YOUR
SMILE
FEET ALWAYS ON A PATH TO
YOUR DOOR. YOU ARE ALL I
CRAVE
MORE.
MORE.
MORE

AS THE DAYS COME AND GO. THE
MOON HASNT LOST ITS ROMANTIC
GLOW. EVEN THOUGH WE ARE NOT
SO YOUNG ANYMORE
WE YET HOLD HANDS AND OUR
HEARTS TOUCH
NOW LUST DOESNT MEAN SO
MUCH
OUR EYES ARE YET SEARCHING
FOR THAT FAMILIAR SMILE . YES
THESE FEET WILL YET WALK A
MILE

FOR THAT PASSIONATE TONGUE
EXPLORING KISS
YEARS HAVE ADDED TO OUR
LOVE BLISS
WE ARE SO CAREFUL TO KEEP THE
FIRE BURNING BRIGHT AND NOT
LET THE EMBERS DIE AS WE
ENTER TWILIGHT
OH YES, THE PASSION FIRE IS YET
THERE AND THE YEARS HAVE
SHOWN US JUST HOW MUCH
WE YET CARE


LDM
11/2003

# YOUNG WOMANS LOVE POEM

I SAW YOU WALKING WITH THAT
BRONZE FRAME OF YOURS
I SAW YOU WALKING THROUGH
MY FRONT DOOR
I THINK OF YOU AS I LAY IN THE
DARK
I CAN FEEL MY HEART BEATING
TIME WITH YOUR HEART
YOU TALK ABOUT THE PAIN FROM
RELATIONSHIP THROUGH THE
YEARS
COME TO ME ILL DRY YOUR
TEARS AND CALM YOUR FEARS
ILL BE WAITING FOR YOUR CALL
ILL CATCH YOU WHEN YOU FALL

I CAN FEEL YOU IN MY ARMS ALL
NIGHT LONG
I CAN SEE YOU SMILING I CAN
HEAR YOU WHISTLING
I CAN HEAR YOU SINGING A SONG__
I CAN FEEL YOU IN MY ARMS ALL
NIGHT LONG

THERE IS PAIN IN YOUR VOICE
UNDERSTAND THE WORDS OF THIS
YOUNG WOMANS LOVE POEM AND
YOU WILL MAKE THE RIGHT
CHOICE

I CAN SEE YOU WALKING WITH
THAT BRONZE FRAME OF YOURS
I CAN SEE YOU WALKING THROUGH
MY FRONT DOOR
I CAN HEAR YOU SINGING ME A
LOVE SONG AS I HOLD YOU IN MY
ARMS ALL NIGHT LONG

# STRENGTH VS COURAGE

I THINK OF YOU NIGHT AND DAY
YOU ARE EMBEDDED IN MY SOUL
SOMEONE ILL ALWAYS LOVE
ONE I WILL NEVER HOLD

WHEN I SEE YOU IM TORN INSIDE
SO I HOLD TIGHTLY TO MY
SUPERFICIAL LOVER .
LOOK AT HIM AND SMILE AS I
WALK BY HIS SIDE
OF MY LIFE YOU ARE SUCH A
PART. TO TELL YOU OF MY
FEELINGS
I DONT KNOW WHERE TO START
SO___ TO MY SUPERFICIAL LOVER

I OPEN MY LEGS AND
CLOSE MY HEART___
I OPEN MY LEGS AND CLOSE MY
HEART

IM TOUGH NOT BRAVE
I THINK OF YOU NIGHT AND DAY
YOU ARE EMBEDDED IN MY SOUL
SOMEONE I WILL A WAYS LOVE
SOMEONE I WILL ALWAYS HOLD

IF I TELL YOU OF MY FEELINGS
YOU MIGHT LAUGH SO I KEEP YOU
IN MY HEART
CONTINUE TO BE A TEMPORARY
PLEASURE A SLAVE
IM TOUGH NOT BRAVE

LDM
01 04-04

65

## LOVE IS AGELELSS

SO MANY YEARS I SPENT NOT
KNOWING WHAT WAS TRUE
ONE DAY I OPENED MY HEART AND
IN STEPPED YOU
YOU ENTERED MY LIFE LIKE A
SOFT SUMMER BREEZE. BRINGING
JOY TO MY HEART AND TO MY
MIND EASE
AS WE LAY HERE READY TO
FULFILL OUR LOVE. OUR HEARTS
ARE ENTWINED. EMOTIONS RUNNING
WILD I HAVE THAT EXCITED
FEELING. ONE I HAVENT FELT IN A
WHILE
AGE DOES NOT MATTER. THOUGHTS
OF IT ONLY DEFEAT
IN YOU MY LOVE I FIND WHAT
WILL MAKE ME COMPLETE.
YOU SMILE AS YOU HOLD ME.
THERE IS NO NEED FOR WORDS
THE SOUND OF ANYTHING BUT OUR
LOVE WILL GO UNHEARD.

SO COME MY LOVE LET OUR
PASSION UNFOLD
IN OUR HEARTS WE ARE YOUNG
LOVERS TONIGHT
NOTHING HERE IS OLD

LDWM
95

66

# IMAGINATION

WHERE CAN I FIND
THIS PICTURE OF U I HAVE IN MY
MIND?
I SEARCH EVERY PLACE TO FIND A
FACE  FOR THIS PICTURE OF U

I HAVE IN MY MIND ARE YOU AN
EARTHLY BEING OR A BEING FROM
OUTER SPACE
YOU HOLD A MYSTERY
I SEARCH BUT I CAN NEVER
PHYSICALLY SEE THIS PICTURE
OF U I HAVE IN MY MIND

I CAN EVEN SEE YOUR HEART SO
PURE AND CLEAN
NOTHING MORE TRUER I'VE EVER
SEEN

WHERE DO I FIND THIS PICTURE OF
U I HAVE IN MY MIND?


LDM

9/23/08
8:45 AM

## MY EYES

MY EYES ALWAYS GIVE MY HEART
AWAY
MY EYES THEY KNOWJUST WHAT TO
SAY
MY EYES. MY EYES. THEY ALWAYS
GIVE MY HEART AWAY
I AM WITH SOMEONE NEW
WE SEEM TO BE DOING FINE. DEEP IN
MY HEART I KNOW YOU WILL
ALWAYS BE MINE
WHEN I SEE YOU PASSING BY. MY
HEART SKIPS A BEAT
I MAY DEEPLY SIGH. BUT MY EYES.
MY EYES ALWAYS GIVE MY HEART
AWAY
MY EYES. THEY KNOW JUST WHAT
TO SAY
MY EYES. MY EYES THEY ALWAYS
GIVE MY HEART AWAY.

LDM
07-18

68

# YESTERYEAR

COME SIT WITH ME MY DEAR
LETS TALK OF YESTERYEAR
THE CHILDREN ARE GROWN AND ON
THEIR OWN. LETS TALK OF
YESTERYEAR
THROUGH THE YEARS WE DID NOT
OUTGROW ONE ANOTHER. YOU
REMAINED MY FRIEND, MY LOVER
SO, LETS FALL IN LOVE. NO LETS
FALL MADLY IN LOVE ALL OVER
AGAIN
AND
WHEN WE ARE THROUGH WITH TALK
OF YESTERYEAR COME LAY WITH
ME

MY FRIEND
MY LOVER
MY DEAR


LDM
1990

# PROPER PLACE

I PUT YOU IN A CORNER AS IF YOU
WERE AN OLD SHOE
SAYING TO MYSELF 'I WILL RETURN
LATER FOR YOU'
NEVER THINKING OF WHAT YOU
COULD BE
ALL I EVER WANTED WAS
WHATEVER'S BEST FOR ME
I NEVER THOUGHT TO LOOK AROUND.
I NEVER CONSIDERED THE SOMEONE
SPECIAL I HAD FOUND UNTIL ONE
DAY I TURNED AND YOU WERE NO
LONGER THERE
THAT GAVE ME AN AWFUL SCARE
THIS HORRIBLE FEAR GRIPPED ME
WHEN I REALIZED YOU WERE GONE
I NEVER FELT SO LOST AND ALONE
NOW WHEN I LOOK AT THAT CORNER
ALL I SEE IS EMPTY SPACE
AS I SIT HERE WITH MYSELF I WISH
I HAD PUT YOU IN ANOTHER PLACE

LDM

## ?

WHEN DID YOU STOP LOVING ME?
WAS IT ON A WINTER EVE WITH
SNOWFLAKES FALLING DOWN

WHEN DID YOU STOP LOVING ME?
WAS IT ON A CLOUDY NIGHT WITH
NO MOON IN THE SKY OR WAS IT
WHEN THE SEA WAS ROLLING AND
NO SHIPS WERE PASSING BY

WHEN DID YOU STOP LOVING ME?
WAS IT ON A SUMMER NIGHT WITH
A FALLING STAR OR DID YOU STOP
LOVING ME BECAUSE YOU ARE
AFRAID OF WHO YOU ARE

WHEN DID YOU STOP LOVING ME?


LDM

# NOTHING LEFT

YOU NO LONGER HOLD ME
STRANGERS WE HAVE BECOME
WHERE IS THE CLOSENESS THAT
ONCE MADE US ONE?

YOU NO LONGER SPEAK TO ME WITH
TENDERNESS IN YOUR VOICE YOUR
TOUCH THAT WAS ONCE GENTLE HAS
BECOME SO HARD AND COARSE

THE SMILE THAT WAS ONCE SO
SPECIAL TO ME I NO LONGER SEE

IT WOULD BE SO MUCH KINDER IF
YOU WOULD GO TO THAT SOMEONE
ELSE BECAUSE YOU CANT HIDE IT
YOUR ACTIONS TELL ME THERE IS

NOTHING LEFT

LDM
93

# U AND I

THE YEARS I SPENT WERE TRUE FOR
ME NOT FOR YOU

THE ANGER I FEEL IS NOT FOR YOU
ITS FOR ME

I WASNT SO BLIND I COULD NOT SEE
IT WAS BECAUSE WHAT I SAW I
WOULD NOT BELIEVE SO NOW LET US
FEEL RELIEVED

THE TIES FOR US HAVE BEEN BROKEN
SO MANY WORDS THAT NEEDED TO
HAVE BEEN WERE NEVER SPOKEN

TIME WILL BANISH THE PAIN I FEEL
THE HEARTACHE WILL SOMEDAY
HEAL

FOR NOW I WILL DO THE BEST FOR
ME AND HOPE THE BEST FOR YOU


LDM
'94

# BE GONE

LONG, TALL MAN
YOU ARE SO FINE
IT MIGHT HAVE BEEN NICE IF YOU
WERE A LOVER OF MINE
ILL BE GONE BEFORE YOU GET HERE

DARK SKINNED MAN WITH A SMILE
SO BRIGHT
ALL SO MYSTERIOUS AS MIDNIGHT
I COULD HAVE ROCKED YOUR WORLD
ALRIGHT
ILL BE GONE BEFORE YOU GET HERE

LOOK AT THAT GREEN-EYED MAN
SO SMOOTH, SO TAN
OH WHAT A TWINKLE IN HIS EYE.
WE COULD HAVE SOARED TO THE
SKY
ILL BE GONE BEFORE YOU GET HERE

THERES THIS LIGHT-SKINNED MAN
FROM ARKANSAS WITH THE
SMOOTHEST STYLE YOU EVER SAW
A SLIGHT GAP BETWEEN HIS FRONT
TEETH, BUT OH HIS LIPS ARE SO, SO
SWEET
FROM WHISKEY, WOMEN AND
GAMBLING, HE CANNOT HIMSELF KEEP
I SHOULD BE GONE WHEN HE GETS
HERE.
LORD YES, I SHOULD BE GONE WHEN
HE GETS HERE

LDM
'93

75

# THAT YELLOW ROSE

OH THAT YELLOW ROSE WHICH
GUARDS MY GARDEN GATE OH THAT
YELLOW ROSE

THAT YELLOW ROSE ITS COLOR IS
AS BRIGHT AS THE SUNLIGHT
BECKONING A NEW DAY
THAT YELLOW ROSE AS GOLDEN AS
THE MOONLIGHT WHICH CHASED MY
BLUES AWAY

OH THAT YELLOW ROSE WHICH
GUARDS MY GARDEN GATE OH THAT
YELLOW ROSE

I GAVE MY LOVE A YELLOW ROSE
JUST THE OTHER DAY I GAVE MY
LOVE A YELLOW ROSE A WORD I
DID NOT SAY
OH THAT YELLOW ROSE WHICH
GUARDS MY GARDEN GATE
OH THAT YELLOW ROSE


LDM
94

# APART

I SEE YOU EACH DAY AS YOU PASS
BY
YOU WERE ONCE MINE. WE GREW SO
FAR APART WITH THE SPANNING
TIME

HOW COULD YOU STOP LOVING ME?
AND TURN TO SOMEONE ELSE. I LONG
FOR US TO GROW OLD TOGETHER
NOW I AM ALONE ALL BY MYSELF

I DREAMED SOMEDAY WE WOULD
TRAVEL THE WORLD FAR AND WIDE
WITH YOU MY LOVE ALWAYS BY
MY SIDE

NOW A BROKEN BEING I SIT
NOT KNOWING WHERE TO START
EACH DAY I LONG TO HOLD YOU IN
MY ARMS. AS I HOLD YOU IN MY
HEART

LDM
94

# TEMPORARY LOVER

WHISPER TO ME SWEET WORDS OF
LOVE. LET MY HEART TAKE FLIGHT
KISS ME. HOLD ME. THRILL ME UNTIL
THE MORNING LIGHT
WHEN THE SUN RISES AND DRIES OFF
THE DEW. A FADING MEMORY IS ALL
ILL HAVE OF YOU
YOU ARE A FORBIDDEN PLEASURE I
HAVE LEARNED TO TREASURE ONE
THAT I BORROW FOR A WHILE NOT
INTENDING TO KEEP
SOMEONE TO HOLD WHEN THE NIGHT
IS COLD AND ITS HARD FOR ME TO
SLEEP
YOU MIGHT RETURN AGAIN. I DONT
KNOW WHEN OR___
MAYBE ILL CHOOSE ANOTHER FOR A
TEMPORARAY LOVER
ILL NOT BECOME ATTACHED___
THERES NO REASON I SEE
THERE IS MORE PLEASURE IN A
TEMPORARAY LOVER

LDM
05/23/02

# LAST NIGHT AND THE NIGHTS BEFORE

I CRIED AGAIN
LAST NIGHT AS I LAY
ON MY BED OF STONE
MY PILLOW OF SOFT DOWN
BECAME A SPONGE FOR
THE FLUID THAT
FLOWED OUT OF MY SOUL THAT CAME
FROM MY HEART THROUGH MY EYES

YES___
LAST NIGHT AGAIN
I CRIED AS I DID THE
NIGHT BEFORE
AND BEFORE.
AND BEFORE.
AND BEFORE.
AND BEFORE___

LDM

# A FOUR LETTER WORD

FOUR LITTLE LETTERS THAT CARRY SO MUCH POWER
THOSE FOUR LETTERS WILL CAUSE:

OUR TONGUE TO STICK TO THE ROOF OF OUR MOUTH
OUR THROAT TO BECOME DRY
OUR LIPS TO FEEL AS PARCHED AS THE ARIZONA DESERT
OUR HEART TO BEAT RAPIDLY
OUR PALMS SWEAT
OUR KNEES SEEM LIKE WATER
OUR EYES FILL WITH TEARS
OFTENTIMES IT WILL ISOLATE, DESOLATE, RENDER US
UNABLE TO CONCENTRATE

FOUR LITTLE LETTERS THAT CAN BIND UP WOUNDS, HEAL
BROKEN HEARTS
OPEN. SHUT. MEND. TEAR. HURT. SEND. BRING

THERE ARE NO OTHER LETTERS WHEN PLACED TOGETHER
CAN BE MORE DYNAMIC AS THE LETTERS LOVE
LOVE IS A HEART THING. LOVE IS A FLOWERING WORD.
LOVE WILL TRAVEL FREELY IN THE BLOODSTREAM IT CAN
BE DEFINED IN MOST ALL OF THE SENSES

LOVE CAN BE HEARD. LOVE CAN BE SEEN. LOVE CAN BE
FELT. LOVE CAN BE TASTED.
IN ITS ACTIVE STATE, LOVE CAN BE SO MUCH IN SUCH
LITTLE TIME

LOVE CAN BE A HEALING BALM TO THE LAND
LOVE THERE IS NOTHING LIKE IT
LETS MAKE LOVE GENUINE

LDM

# LaDora White McDaniel

## "LaDee"

LaDora White McDaniel was born
August 31, 1945 in St. Louis, MO.
LaDora was educated at the
Palestine, AR school grades 1-8
and grades 9-12 at the Lincoln
High School in Forrest City, AR
where she graduated in 1963.
She worked for 40+ years but
never lost the Voice in Her Hand.
LaDora ascended to heaven in
2020 without ever seeing her art
reach the masses. She had dreams
of one day publishing her craft
and that time is NOW!

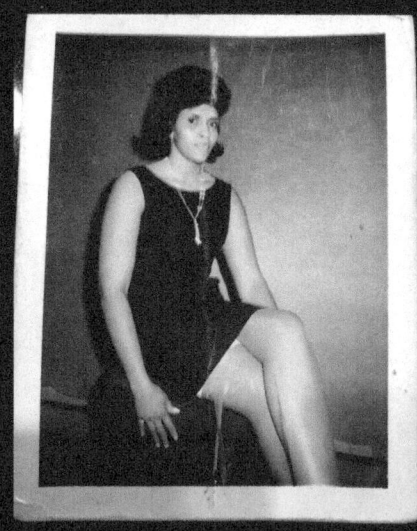

leiaslegacybooks@yahoo.com

Thank you to all who helped bring this to fruition

Made in the USA
Coppell, TX
21 January 2026

68857762R00049